The Essential

Executive

By the same author

Real Medicine: The A–Z Guide
White Knights and Poison Pills
(with David Olive)

The Essential

Executive

Edited by
PAUL STEVENSON

ROBERT HALE · LONDON

© Paul Stevenson 1995
First published in Great Britain 1995

ISBN 0 7090 5307 X

Robert Hale Limited
Clerkenwell House
Clerkenwell Green
London EC1R 0HT

2   4   6   8   10   9   7   5   3   1

Photoset in Century Schoolbook by
Derek Doyle & Associates, Mold, Clwyd.
Printed in Hong Kong

Preface

The three hundred inhabitants of Crosshaven were puzzled by an application to build eighty executive homes near their village. 'I didn't know there were that many executives living here,' said Wesley Crawford, County Cork's urbane equivalent of Harry Ramsden. Would this mean an influx of eighty mobile phones, eighty Porsches and a branch of Quaglino's beside the Credit Union?

The speculation led to attempts to define terms. What actually is an executive? Is that person over there behind the pot plant one, or a mere manager? Are you one, possibly unawares? If not, how could you become one, and how would you know when you had?

To be an *executant* suggests some form of acquired expertise; to be an *executor* or *executrix* suggests a recent death; but an *executive*, according to *Chambers*, is one 'designed or fitted to execute or perform' – something between a hangman and a stand-up comic. Fair enough, but executives are also people who can travel to any part of the world with only one telephone call, who get paid to eat free lunches, and are always busy, even when asleep on a plane.

At the top, they run corporations with larger budgets than some nation states, consort with presidents and prime ministers, serve prison sentences for fraud, hold press conferences to announce their views on macro-economics, stand for political office, donate shareholders' cash to photogenic charities, and collect honours and titles for so doing.

On the way up or on the way down, they are largely interchangeable with ordinary people, whether running double-glazing companies, constructing business plans, lunching with journalists, stringing abstract nouns together into motivating slogans, swapping a spouse of forty for two twenties, negotiating joint ventures, or just Doing Important Things. Separate these middle- and lower-range executives from their secretaries, cars and expense accounts – on holiday or to redundancy counselling perhaps – and they revert to being just ordinary people with ordinary problems, like paying bills and finding somewhere to park.

Top executives, however, are different. Top executives are always top executives, even when top judges have sent them to top prisons for stealing from top companies. No top executive is ever so bankrupt that frequent first-class flights on Concorde are a problem.

But is not the executive life in the nasty nineties rough, tough, high-tech and demanding? Do not ulcers and heart attacks go with the territory? Not always. True, the life can be hectic if you are an advertising executive in the middle of a major launch, or a finance executive in an acquisition frenzy; but, for most of their careers, few executives dash away from their offices like process workers the moment the clock reaches its appointed hour. Most linger. They would rather stay a little longer in the warm matrix of their office, performing some arcane substitute activity, than return immediately to a commissionaire-less home, waiter-less meals, deference-free relationships and demands to mend punctures on muddy mountain bikes.

This book looks at the Essential Executive from the inside out; what they say about themselves, their colleagues, products, competitors, enemies, and what others say about them. Not all the quotations are *by* executives,

but they are all *for* executives, and, because
good quotations contain their own authority,
they should be useful for dropping into
conversations and communications, peror-
ations and presentations.

They reflect a journalist's lifetime habit of
reading almost everything (*except library
books*) with either scissors or a pen in hand,
filing whatever makes one hoot with amuse-
ment, gasp at chutzpah, groan at pompousness
or exclaim at shrewdness. This noisy process
has provided such riches that I have been
emboldened to leave out as many as possible of
what have now become the standby cliché-
quotations from such stars as Oscar Wilde,
Mark Twain, Sir Winston Churchill and
William Shakespeare. However, in exercising
this iron self-control I may have left out both of
your favourite executive quotations. Sorry.

Some of the present-day financial quotations,
like the Abbey National explanation of the
superiority of equities over stocks and shares,
were phoned or faxed in, though their mischie-
vous tone suggests a mole in *Money Marketing*,
that essential pink tabloid taken by endan-
gered insurance brokers. Thanks to all
concerned.

So here is the Essential Executive life, as
illumined by representatives of the BBC, the
official Mafia, Barclays de Zoete Wedd, Pearl
Insurance, Betterware and Saatchi and

Saatchi; as expounded by such executives as Donald Trump, Ross Goobey, John Birt, Robert Maxwell and Adolf Hitler; as quoted in *The Sunday Times, The Charleston Gazette, The New York Times, Mainichi Daily News* and *Woman's Realm*; and as reproved by Chinese, American, Jewish and Zulu proverbs. Here, too, is the truth about free lunches.

Incidentally, when those Crosshaven executive homes were finally occupied, it was by disappointingly ordinary people – like many boardrooms, actually.

Paul Stevenson
Teignmouth

We have been transformed from an organization that rates alongside the BBC, into a bunch of greedy, money-grabbing barons who don't give a damn about television or its quality.

SENIOR ITV EXECUTIVE

It's the Virtual Reality Senior Management Simulator. You pee into the dark, pray to God you hit the right spot, and nine times out of ten, come out with a wet leg.

BBC EXECUTIVE QUOTED IN *THE TIMES*
when the lights in staff lavatories were
removed as an economy measure

I do not wish to absolutely accept that as a fair and complete characterization of the organization in all places at all times

JOHN BIRT
Director-General of the BBC
responding to staff criticisms

We've got executives who get paid more to plan the news than the Prime Minister gets to make it.

BBC EXECUTIVE
radio interview

We would like to welcome back long-wave listeners and apologise for the 20-minute break in transmission. We hope it didn't spoil your enjoyment of *Thirty Minute Theatre*.

BBC RADIO 4 ANNOUNCER

When the boss tells you to do something, you do it. You don't do it, they kill you.

> ALADENA 'JIMMY THE WEASEL' FRATIANNO
> of Carmine 'The Snake' Persico, 'Fat Tony'
> Salerno, Johnny 'The Rope' Roselli and John
> 'Blackie' Licavori, his fellow American business
> executives.

He was a symbol of Italy.

> SENATOR VIOLANTE
> of Italian industrialist Raul Gardini, who shot
> himself while under investigation on
> corruption charges.

I do unto others what they do unto me, only worse.

> JIMMY HOFFA
> union executive

If two wrongs don't make a right, try three.

> DR LAURENCE J. PETER
> in *The Peter Principle*

My father told me that all businessmen were sons-of-bitches, but I never believed him until now.

> JOHN F. KENNEDY
> US President and Pulitzer prize winner

We need safeguards against arbitrary cancell-ation of the employment contract by the employer. The law has a duty to protect the weaker in a contractual relationship and to constrain the more powerful from the abuse of his advantage.

PETER DRUCKER
The Age of Discontinuity

Excessive turnover [of staff] in any industry or at any period is a bad thing socially, reflecting a poor state of morale or unsatisfactory relations between the parties in industry.

C.H. NORTHCOTT
Personnel Management

Much British management doesn't understand the human factor.

PRINCE CHARLES

Rare is the executive who can weigh the faults of his colleagues without putting his thumb on the scale.

CHINESE PROVERB

If you have nothing to say, or, rather, something extremely stupid and obvious, say it, but in a 'plonking' tone of voice – i.e. roundly, but hollowly and dogmatically.

STEPHEN POTTER
Lifemanship

A principle isn't a principle until it costs you money.

STEPHEN CHIPPERFIELD
Hill Murray

Most bankers live in marble halls
Which they get to dwell in because they
    encourage deposits and discourage
    withdralls,
And particularly because they observe one
    rule which woe betides the bankers who
    fail to heed it,
Which is never to lend money to anybody
    unless they don't need it.
OGDEN NASH

The difference between a dead skunk and a dead banker on the road is that there are skid marks by the dead skunk.
ANON

Why do they call them tellers? They never tell you anything. They just ask questions. And why do they call it interest? It's boring. And another thing – how come the Trust Department has all their pens chained to the table?
NBC TV'S *CHEERS*

There is no point in not welcoming another cut in interest rate, because the Chancellor is not going to consult me.
DONALD KIRKHAM
Woolwich Building Society
declining a press interview

I like our managed fund. It's safer than some because it has more equities than stocks and shares.

ABBEY NATIONAL EXECUTIVE

Sell Rome, buy gnome.

BARCLAYS DE ZOETE WEDD
executive advice on investing in Italy and
Switzerland

In the kingdom of the one-eyed, he would rob you blind.

Traditional, attributed to SAM GOLDWYN

Robert Maxwell says he'll only allow his sons Ian and Kevin to take over his vast empire if they are capable. 'Money you haven't earned isn't good for you,' he claims. His children won't automatically benefit from his fortune, he says, because he's already given them a good start in life.

WOMAN'S REALM
20 August 1991

There is nothing the British like more than a bloke who comes from nowhere, makes it, and then gets clobbered.

MELVYN BRAGG
Rich, a biography of Richard Burton

This bankruptcy has been described as the world's biggest, but really it is a very ordinary bankruptcy with noughts at the end.

ALAN SALES
Official Receiver, of the 1978 failure of William Stern

The main parts of the verb 'to fail' are: fail, failed, bankrupt.

THE EDUCATION OF H*Y*M*A*N   K*A*P*L*A*N

When we come to that bridge, we'll jump off it.

TRADITIONAL

The day you take complete responsibility for yourself, the day you stop making any excuses, that's the day you start to the top.

O.J. SIMPSON
sports personality and courtroom star

You will find as you look back upon your life that the moments when you have really lived, are the moments when you have done things in a spirit of love.

HENRY DRUMMOND

He had no ears for any charity unless labelled with his name. He would have given millions to Greece had she labelled the Parthenon 'Carnegopolis'.

> POULTNEY BIGELOW
> of American multi-millionaire Andrew
> Carnegie's notorious self-publicizing

Man does not live by words alone, despite the fact that he sometimes has to eat them.

> ADLAI STEVENSON
> American presidential contender and author

His curiosity is huge, his information is shallow, derived from conversations and magazines and newspaper articles – material he can digest quickly. On most matters he is shallow, resorting to analogy, anecdote and carefully selected statistics rather than relying on a complex and detailed knowledge of the subject.

> ROBERT SOBEL
> on financier Michael Milken in *Dangerous Dreamers*

Were they [the much-admired corporate raiders] really Robin Hood and his Merry Men, as they claimed? Or were they Genghis Khan and his Mongol hordes? ... I don't see the raiders creating jobs. I don't see them boosting productivity. And worst of all, I don't see them doing a single thing to help America compete in the world.

LEE IACOCCA
American industrialist and writer

Michael Milken, another Wall Street manipulator, was fined $600,000,000 for his junk-bond dealings – he made almost that much in one year! He was able to retain $1,500,000,000.

AWAKE!
January 1992

So here's to greed!

IVAN BOESKY
in a business-school speech before being jailed and fined $100,000,000 (they allegedly let him keep the other $500,000,000)

Only the uninformed get caught.

AUGIE WOLD
US shot-putter
quoted in *Newsweek*

It is generally considered more comfortable to take a dog's tail off all at once, rather than an inch at a time.

CHARLES BROWN
chairman of AT&T, explaining their $5.2 billion write-offs in 1983

He heard himself assailed as a self-centred financial executive who buttered his own beard.

EARLE TEMPLE
More Press Boners

I'm going out for our office lunch, and I'm not taking calls this afternoon.

STEWART RICHIE
Scottish Equitable

Calamities are of two kinds: misfortunes to ourselves, and good fortune to others.

AMBROSE BIERCE
The Devil's Dictionary

To some [executives], money means security. To some it means power. To others it means they're going to be able to buy love, and to a fourth group it means competition and winning the game.

JAY ROHRLICH
psychiatrist
quoted in *The Watchtower*

Whatever the importance of money, none could doubt the importance of the fears it engendered.

J.K. GALBRAITH

The newly rich executives of the 1980s want something for nothing: the most amount of money with the least amount of effort.

MACLEAN'S MAGAZINE

The business people of [ancient Babylon] ... carried on a surprisingly complex system of lending, borrowing, holding money on deposit, and providing letters of credit.

THE ENCYCLOPAEDIA AMERICANA

The centuries that followed [500 BC] were so marked by the development of trade, money, banks, transport, that several historians have compared them to the capitalist era.

THE COLLINS ATLAS OF WORLD HISTORY

Stop storing up for yourselves treasures upon the earth, where moth and rust consume, and where thieves break in and steal. Rather, store up for yourselves treasures in heaven, where neither moth nor rust consumes, and where thieves do not break in and steal.

JESUS
Matthew 6:19–20

But here for the first time ... business in itself, money-making in itself, production of goods and heaping up of comforts, assumed such power over man that he spent all of his vitality, his heart, all his present and future, all his human being, in the literal sense of the word, in a restless, a persistently growing and devouring production per se, a production, the final

21

meaning of which he has completely lost and forgotten.

ERICH KAHLER
of Jakob Fugger, medieval executive for the
Pope

In our culture we make heroes of men who sit on top of a heap of money, and we pay attention not only to what they say in their field of competence, but to their wisdom on every other question in the world.

MAX LERNER
journalist
1949

Merchants are replacing warriors as the main actors on the world stage.

JACQUES ATTALI
French presidential adviser

One [executive], who came into work one morning to find that his desk had been moved, climbed up to the top of the building and jumped off.

US NEWS & WORLD REPORT

They keep asking me to send them jiffy bags stuffed with money.

DAVID THOMAS
chairman of Surewater Group
of the executives of a recently acquired
company

Men who pass most comfortably through the world are those who possess good digestions and hard hearts.

HARRIET MARTINEAU

Physical inactivity doubles the risk of heart attack, and researchers classify sedentary people in the same high-risk category for heart attacks as smokers and people with high blood pressure or high cholesterol levels.

BOARDROOM REPORTS
December 1988

The world continues to offer glittering prizes to those who have stout hearts and sharp swords.

F.E. SMITH (EARL OF BIRKENHEAD)
1923

Try to remember that work cannot be the only thing in life.
> BILL CLINTON
> US President
> after suspected suicide of his aide and friend
> Vincent Foster jun.

We are none of us infallible, not even the youngest of us.
> WILLIAM THOMPSON
> Fellow of Trinity
> referring to G.W. Ballantyne, junior fellow of
> Trinity

In March, BP revealed that ousting Bob Horton as chairman last year cost £1.5m; during Horton's tenure the company reported its first-ever quarterly loss, and its share price fell almost 25%.
> MATTHEW LYNN
> *The Sunday Times*, June 1993

Too often recently we have read of senior executives who have been deemed to have failed in their role but, as a consequence of their contract, have been paid off with substantial sums.
> ROSS GOOBEY
> chief executive of Postel

There were some very obvious superficial signals that the company had lost touch with its business. The annual report was full of sportsmen wearing Spring Ram shirts, but there were no pictures of bathrooms.

TERRY SMITH
analyst
on troubled bathrooms group Spring Ram

While this month Invesco admitted 55 charges of breaching City regulations and was fined £750,000 plus £1.6m costs [Lord] Stevens has departed from Invesco with a £75,000 pay-off and his £300,000 salary paid up to September.

THE SUNDAY TIMES

The sentence on Roger Levitt is nothing better than a sick joke. It will do nothing to deter others and will merely infuriate his victims.

JOHN MARSHALL
MP for Hendon South
on insurance executive Levitt's sentence of 180
hours community service following his
company's £34-million failure

There must be hundreds of people in the City laughing their heads off and saying, 'Look at what we can get away with.'

MICHAEL WINNER

The gambling known as business looks with austere disfavour upon the business known as gambling.

AMBROSE BIERCE

Business is a combination of war and sport.

ANDRÉ MAUROIS

I don't want a lawyer to tell me what I cannot do; I hire him to tell me how to do what I want to do.

J. PIERPOINT MORGAN

The two richest men in the world make motor cars and sell the gas for them, but the people maintain the emergency hospitals.

CHARLESTON GAZETTE
on Henry Ford and John Rockefeller

One can fight evil but against stupidity one is helpless.

ARTHUR MILLER
On Turning Eighty

He was Euclid's definition of a point – he had no parts, and no magnitude, but he had position.

WILLIAM THOMPSON
of a titled blockhead

Howard Hughes, America's bashful billionaire, epitomises the dilemma of twentieth-century America; inventive, brilliant, fantastic, overwhelming in technical precocity and accomplishment – suspicious, complex, contradictory, and sometimes downright antediluvian in social outlook.

ALBERT B. GERBER

His talents are always there – but most of the time they're lying doormat. Comes a challenge – and *ah*! His true worth rises to the surface like – like a cornplaster when you're having a bath.

FRANK MUIR AND DENIS NORDEN
Mr Glum of his executive potential son Ronald
Crippen Glum in *Take it from Here*

It has ... been said that there are few situations in life that cannot be honourably settled, and without loss of time, either by suicide, a bag of gold, or by thrusting a despised antagonist over the edge of a precipice on a dark night.

ERNEST BRAMAH

The best portion of a man's life: his little nameless unremembered acts of kindness and love.

WILLIAM WORDSWORTH

I did it because I want to see your dead body floating down the river as an example to enemies of the state.

> TRISTAN GAREL-JONES
> MP
> on the sacking of Edward Leigh. Widely quoted after boardroom battles

When you call me that, *smile*.

> OWEN WISTER
> in *The Virginian* (1960s' TV series)

It is one of the most beautiful compensations of this life that no man can sincerely try to help another without helping himself.

> RALPH WALDO EMERSON

Men might live quiet and easy enough, if they would be careful not to give themselves trouble, and forbear meddling with what other people do and say, in which they are in no way concerned.

> THOMAS À KEMPIS

Let sleeping ducks lie.

> Traditional, attributed to SAM GOLDWYN

From ancient times, there has been talk of the human mind being a part of a greater mind, i.e., the Universal Subconscious Mind, the Collective Unconscious, the Supraconscious, the

Infinite Intelligence, etc. ... We all have a Superconscious Mind that we constantly use, often in a haphazard way.

> BRIAN TRACY
> American executive motivator

The Understanding Process wraps us all around and holds us together in a team of teams. It begins and ends in a sense back at the beginning.

> KAREN McCORMICK
> *The Manager Of The Understanding Process*,
> National and Provincial Building Society

Any security based on the good will and common sense of others is worthless, as there is as little good and faithfulness in other men as there is in you (and you know how little that is).

> US BANK EXECUTIVE
> quoted by Dwight Skelton

Wealth has never been a sufficient source of honour in itself. It must be advertised, and the normal medium is obtrusively expensive goods.

> J.K. GALBRAITH

The belief that money can produce these things ... often leads to impotence, insomnia, heart attacks and problems with a spouse or children.

> *SCIENCE DIGEST*

Can't executives earning $100,000 a year afford to buy their own cars? You don't understand, respond the experts; it's not a question of affording, it's a question of being loved.

FORTUNE

Money is the most important thing in the world. It represents health, strength, honour, generosity, and beauty as conspicuously as the want of it represents illness, weakness, disgrace, meanness, and ugliness ... it destroys base people as certainly as it fortifies and dignifies noble people.

GEORGE BERNARD SHAW

Money is human happiness in the abstract: he, then, who is no longer capable of enjoying human happiness in the concrete devotes himself utterly to money.

ARTHUR SCHOPENHAUER

Money is paper blood.

BOB HOPE

My observations suggest that the more successful the businessman, the more unethical the behaviour.

UTAH CONSULTANT
in *Industry Week*

Our policy is if you can get away with it, do it.

MIAMI EXECUTIVE
in *Industry Week*

There's no use looking for excuses or extenuating circumstances why people take or pay bribes. They do it because they like money – period.

ANTONIA DI PIETRO
prosecutor in the Sergio Cusani £60-million bribe trial

Shower upon him every blessing, drown him in a sea of happiness, give him economic prosperity such that he would have nothing to do but sleep, eat cakes, and busy himself with the continuation of his species; and even then, out of sheer ingratitude, sheer spite, man would play you some nasty trick.

F.M. DOSTOEVSKY

If wealth does not give happiness, poverty will; if learning does not solve everything, then true wisdom will lie in ignorance.

ORTEGA Y GASSET
Spanish philosopher

Nothing knits man to man like the frequent passage of cash from hand to hand.

WALTER SICKERT
Anglo–German artist

We do not have to acquire humility. There is humility in us – only we humiliate ourselves before false gods.

> SIMONE WEIL
> French philosopher and religious writer

Life in our house was one long board meeting. We kids understood where the money came from – we were taken to visit the factories.

> DAME SHIRLEY PORTER of the Tesco family
> interviewed by Lesley White

Don't bite the hand that lays the golden egg.

> LONDON JEWISH PROVERB

There's no reason to be the richest man in the cemetery. You can't do any business from there.

> COLONEL SANDERS

I don't know anyone who wished on his deathbed that he had spent more time in the office.

> PETER LYNCH
> US investment superstar
> quoted in *Awake!*

Business underlies everything in our national life, including our spiritual life. Witness the fact that in the Lord's Prayer the first petition is for daily bread. No-one can love his neighbour or worship God on an empty stomach.

WOODROW WILSON
US President

There's nothing in Christianity or Buddhism that quite matches the sympathetic unselfishness of an oyster.

SAKI
The Quest

Business is like oil. It won't mix with anything else.

J. GRAHAM

No men can act with effect who do not act in concert; no men can act in concert who do not act with confidence; no men can act in confidence who are not bound together with common opinions, common affections and common interests.

EDMUND BURKE

People of the same trade seldom meet together, even for merriment or diversion, but the conversation ends in a conspiracy against the public, or in some contrivance to raise prices.

ADAM SMITH
The Wealth of Nations

The way in which the West Bromwich has behaved has been utterly scandalous, deeply shocking and would certainly merit much closer investigation, particularly by the police.

> WILLIAM POWELL
> MP for Corby
> on some West Bromwich Building Society
> home income plans

Those of us in this House who have tried to seek some small measure of justice for our constituents have met a brick wall.

> WILLIAM POWELL
> MP for Corby
> bravely, on the same failed home income plans

He has done a good job. I happen to know that when he took over, your institution was on the edge of a precipice. Under his direction, it has taken a giant step forward.

> PETER JOSLIN
> chief constable of Warwickshire
> on Charles Dickie, president of the Chartered
> Building Societies Institute

An executive is handed a written report; he pushes it aside and says, 'I've no time to wade through all that garbage. Tell me about it in your own words – briefly.' If the subordinate comes in with a verbal suggestion, this man chokes him off in mid-sentence with, 'I can't even begin to think about it until you put it in writing.'

DR LAURENCE J. PETER
in *The Peter Principle*

Always mistrust a subordinate who never finds fault with his superior.

JOHN CHURTON COLLINS
English scholar and critic
in *Voltaire, Montesquieu and Rosseau in England*

The trouble with senior management to an outsider is that there are too many one-ulcer men holding down two-ulcer jobs.

PRINCE PHILIP

The rear wheels of commerce are worth a dollar each.

CHEYENNE WYOMING STATE TRIBUNE
quoted by Colin Jarman

Here lies one who meant well, tried a little, failed much: – surely that may be his epitaph, of which he need not be ashamed.

ROBERT LOUIS STEVENSON

I don't see why they call it a level playing field anyway. What do they think we do all day? We work, not play.

FRANK ATTRILL
chief executive of Scottish Widows
on the Financial Services Act, a long-running farce

Ninety-nine percent of managing directors of large companies are male; ninety-nine percent of chief executives in local authorities are male. Ninety-seven percent of trade union general secretaries are male. Women form forty-three percent of the labour force. Their wages average one-third less than men's.

LABOUR RESEARCH DEPARTMENT
1992

I have been what the US relocation jargon calls a trailing spouse – i.e. those of us who are relocated because of the other half's career move.

JOANNA FOSTER
chair of the Equal Opportunities Commission

If the good Lord had intended us all to have equal rights to go out to work and to behave equally, you know he really wouldn't have created man and woman.

PATRICK JENKIN
MP, later Secretary of State for Social Services

In point of morals, the average woman is, even for business, too crooked.

STEPHEN LEACOCK
Humorist and lecturer in economics

Men are never so tired and harassed as when they deal with a woman who wants a raise.

MICHAEL KORDA

Women always ran the show. They were level-headed. They had to cope with day-to-day reality. Men go off on these flights of fancy.

SHUSHA GUPPY
writer and singer, on Asian business life
quoted in *Style and Travel*

Women have served all these centuries as looking glasses possessing the ... power of reflecting the figure of man at twice its natural size.

VIRGINIA WOOLF

I do not wish [women] to have power over men; but over themselves.

MARY WOLLSTONECRAFT

To be successful, a woman has to be better at her job than a man.

GOLDA MEIR
former Prime Minister of Israel

Whatever women do they must do twice as well as men to be thought half as good. Luckily, this is not difficult.

CHARLOTTE WHITTON
Entrepreneur

Give a woman a job and she grows balls.

JACK GERBER

You can't sit back and be some venerable bloody rhetorician … you've got to *do* and show how it can be done.

ANITA RODDICK
chief executive of the Body Shop
interviewed by *Lear's* magazine, New York

She realised that she was not cut out for the hand-to-hand fighting that was necessary, and decided instead to follow Peer Gynt when, faced with the Great Boyg, he was told 'You must go round.'

BERNARD LEVIN

Perhaps what every man over thirty who has sat shiftily through the week's proceedings now needs is a way of dealing with accumulated guilt. A sexual harassment amnesty.

LAURIE TAYLOR
The Times

She's tough, but has she got the ovaries for the job?

MARIE HUTCHINGS
Scottish executive recruiter

Truly decent people only exist among men with definite convictions; so-called moderates are much drawn to rewards, orders, commissions, promotions.

ANTON CHEKHOV

I think the sheikh is worth about $6 billion, but I don't know for sure because I can't count all the zeroes.

MARVIN MITCHELSON
divorce lawyer and inventor of 'palimony'
on the Sheikh Mohammed al-Fassi divorce

I had an accountant draw up my tax returns and I thought he knew what he was doing and like most busy men I just signed what was put in front of me.

MARVIN MITCHELSON
appealing against a prison term for alleged tax
irregularities
in an interview with Russell Miller

I'm a cross between an accountant and an unconvicted forger.

JOHN B. KEANE
in *The Contractors*

Let's get down to brass roots.
SOUTH WEST WATER EXECUTIVE

Accountancy is one of the most difficult professions for people trying to find dates.
FRANCES PYNE
Dateline executive

A finance director is someone who likes playing with numbers, but lacks the charisma to be an accountant.
PAUL MILLER
financial journalist

He's a pessimist, always building dungeons in the air.
Traditional, attributed to SAM GOLDWYN

If anyone has a new idea in this country, there are twice as many people who advocate putting a man with a red flag in front of it.
PRINCE PHILIP

Free-trade in goods was so simple … that men argued that free-trade in labour between master and workman must be equally bene-ficial … But labour is less fluid; it is attached to a home and is not ready to go hither and thither in pursuit of every trifling rise in wage; it cannot be stored … and in this sense labour is more perishable than any commodity.

> G.T. WARNER
> *Landmarks in English Industrial History*
> 1899

I know all about these problems. I grew up in the thirties with an unemployed father. He didn't riot. He got on his bike and looked for work. And he found it!

> NORMAN TEBBIT
> MP
> at Conservative party conference, 1981

It drags itself out of the abysm of pish, and crawls insanely up the topmost pinnacle of tosh. It is rumble and bumble. It is flap and doodle. It is balder and dash.

> H.L. MENCKEN
> on executive speech

He is a self-made man and worships his creator.

> JOHN BRIGHT
> on Prime Minister Benjamin Disraeli

The best minds are not in government. If any were, business would hire them anyway.

> RONALD REAGAN
> US President

There cannot be a crisis next week. My schedule is already full.

> HENRY KISSINGER
> 1977
> National Security Affairs adviser to US
> President Nixon

Look at me: I worked my way up from nothing to a state of extreme poverty.

GROUCHO MARX
Monkey Business

It's the little things in life that matter, not fame, success, wealth. At the top there's very little room, whereas at the bottom there's plenty like you, no crowding and nobody to egg you on.

HENRY MILLER
On Reaching Eighty

I started at the top, and then I worked down.

ORSON WELLES
executive producer

The key ingredient is that you won't get talented people to work *for* you if they don't get a chance to work *with* you ... The boss who persists with the old fantasies would be well-advised to recognise both the new assertiveness of well-educated employees and that shared decision-making may yield more effective results.

ANTHONY J. ECCLES
Manchester Business School

It took me 25 years to discover I had no talent, but I couldn't give it up because by that time I was famous.

ROBERT BENCHLEY

The toughest thing about success is that you've got to keep on being a success.

IRVING BERLIN

Progress always involves risk; you can't steal second base and keep your foot on first.

FREDRICK WILCOX

I have a fascination with risk. It makes me feel alive. I can get bored just living.

GEORGE SOROS
billionaire currency speculator

Sales executives should be optimists, and credit controllers should be pessimists.

ROGER REGAN

His most favoured hobbies are tennis, golf, eating, chasing women (when he has the energy) and more eating.

CV OF DANNY O'NEILL
Britannia Life Investment Managers

In order to succeed, we must first believe that we can.

MICHAEL KORDA

I do not think there is any other quality so essential to success as the quality of per-severance. It overcomes almost everything, even nature.

JOHN D. ROCKEFELLER

If at first you don't succeed, try again. Then quit. No use being a damn fool about it.
W.C. FIELDS

Back to Basics becomes Back to My Place.
HILL MARTIN (ASSET MANAGEMENT) EXECUTIVE

I'd rather fight my corner and pay for my fight than surrender. If I get done, I'll walk away. At least I'll be able to sleep at night.
TERRY VENABLES
of his relationship with fellow-director Alan
Sugar and Tottenham Hotspur

One chief engineer worked out in the gym every week lifting weights to improve his leadership qualities. Employing a logic all his own, he explained to his colleagues that it was right that he should be chief engineer because he could lift a heavier weight than anyone else.
IVOR CATT
The Catt Concept

The watch-word for Side-Issue Specialists is *Look after the molehills and the mountains will look after themselves*.
DR LAURENCE J. PETER
in *The Peter Principle*

You will become as small as your controlling desire; as great as your dominant aspiration.
JAMES ALLEN
executive motivator

It is sobering to think that when Mozart was my age he had already been dead a year.

TOM LEHRER

A sure sign of recession in the movie industry is when executives of a major studio start laying off relatives.

IRVIN COBB
The Best of Cobb

People always say I shouldn't be burning my candle at both ends. Maybe because they don't have a big enough candle.

GEORGE BEST
West End entrepreneur

The strongest single factor in prosperity consciousness is self-esteem: believing you can do it, believing you deserve it, believing you will get it.

JERRY GILLIES
Executive motivator

If I owe you a dollar, I am in your power; but if I owe you a million dollars, you are in my power.

AMERICAN PROVERB

Recent experience has shown that it is extremely difficult for business executives to judge the soundness of a bank. Practically every large bank that collapsed in recent years, or nearly collapsed, had been highly touted by bank-stock analysts.

THE NEW YORK TIMES

If borrowing from a bank is so easy, why should anyone want to rob it?

ANON

A financier is a pawnbroker with imagination.

SIR ARTHUR PINERO
Playwright in *£200 a Year*

It is anticipated that the portfolio will initially be invested 65% in Europe (including the UK), 35% in the Far East and Australasia, and 10% in emerging markets such as Mexico and Turkey.

GUINNESS FLIGHT EXECUTIVE
on its Global Privatisation Trust

It would be like Marks and Spencer saying they had never sold a pair of knickers with faulty elastic.

KEN McKYE OF PEARL
on claims that the industry would be cleared of bad pension transfer charges

There is a hankering after the spirit of the Wild West, where men were men and one took misfortune and suffering without whimpering.

IVOR CATT

Routine is essential ... [it] frees creative energies for dealing with the more baffling array of new problems for which routinization is an irrational approach.

WILLIAM JAMES
1958
American psychologist

Mesmerised as we are by the very idea of change, we must guard against the notion that continuity is a negligible factor in human history. It is a vitally important ingredient ...

JOHN GARDNER
Self-Renewal

It's tradition. We don't want tradition. We want to live in the present and the only history that is worth a tinker's damn is the history we make today.

HENRY FORD
1916

Any event, once it has occurred, can be made to appear inevitable by a competent historian.

PAUL DICKSON
The Official Rules
1978

Some of you have heard John Ferguson before and some haven't. Those of you who haven't will be looking forward eagerly to hearing him.

> PROFESSOR JOHN FERGUSON
> of a chairman's introduction

An executive is someone who can take as long as he likes to make a snap decision.

> BOB NEWHART
> American humorist

People said they were born executives. What they meant was, Daddy owned the company.

> MIRROR GROUP NEWSPAPERS
> of Robert Maxwell's sons

It is essential that ... the skills of the public relations professional are shown to be above suspicion ... never more so has the integrity of IPR members become so important.

> in July 1993 edition of the Institute of Public
> Relations' organ

Clients want an account executive who is between twenty-five and thirty, with forty years' experience.

> JASON CALLANDER
> chief executive of Consensus Communications

The end of apartheid is opening up South Africa for full-scale PR development.

> *PR WEEK*

Public relations specialists make flower arrangements of the facts, placing them so that the wilted and less attractive petals are hidden by sturdy blooms.
ALAN HARRINGTON

It's a business that develops megalomania … Don't get taken in by all the bullshit.
ROBERT LOUIS-DREYFUS
corporate saver of Saatchi and Saatchi, August 1993

Only constant repetition will finally succeed in imprinting an idea on the memory of the crowd.
ADOLF HITLER

B.A.T. Uganda 1984 Ltd does not believe that cigarette smoking is harmful to health.
STATEMENT BY B.A.T. SPOKESMAN TO MINISTRY OF HEALTH IN ENTEBBE

On CBS radio the news of Ed Murrow's death, reportedly from lung cancer, was followed by a cigarette commercial.
ALEXANDER KENDRICK

You can fool all of the people all of the time if the advertising is right and the budget is big enough.
JOSEPH E. LEVINE

Any man with ambition, integrity – and $10 million – can start a daily newspaper.

HENRY MORGAN

Surviving at the Top – The book's title alone ... is so perversely marvellous that there ought to be a contest to invent others that could equal it ... Marie Antoinette's *Keeping My Head*, Achilles' *Recovering from a Tendon Injury*, General Custer's *Outfoxing the Enemy*, and Jean-Claud Duvallier's *President for Life*.

JOHN ROTHSCHILD
Los Angeles Times
on Donald Trump's oeuvre

Advertisements are now so numerous that they are very negligently perused, and it is therefore become necessary to gain attention by magnificence of promise and by eloquence sometimes sublime and sometimes pathetick.

SAMUEL JOHNSON
1758

Half the money I spend on advertising is wasted, and the trouble is, I don't know which half.

JOHN WANAMAKER
American retailer

Some people have expressed the dark opinion that one of the reasons for *The Times* modernising itself is to get more readers. Of

54

course it is. And we shall go on trying to get more readers for as long as we believe in our purpose.

THE TIMES
leader, 3 May 1966, announcing decision to print news on the front page

Advertising may be described as the science of arresting the human intelligence long enough to get money from it.

STEPHEN LEACOCK

In baiting a mousetrap with cheese, always leave room for the mouse.

SAKI

Being in this business without making calls is like winking at a girl in the dark – you know what you're doing, but she doesn't.

JOHN DAVIES
Allied Dunbar executive

Marketing executives who stop advertising to save money are like people who stop the clock to save time.

PAUL HARVEY
Teignmouth Pioneer

Advertising is what you do when you can't go see somebody.

FAIRFAX CONE

A businessman is the only one who always seeks to make it appear, when he attains the object of his labours, i.e., the making of a great deal of money, that it was not the object of his labours.
H.L. MENCKEN

The broad mass of a nation … will more readily fall victim to a big lie than to a small one.
ADOLF HITLER

Clever liars don't give details.
AMERICAN PROVERB

There is no such thing as a free lunch.
TRADITIONAL LIE
told to each other by thousands of executive free-loaders

Today's customer has given two fingers to the designer decade; they want an honest product.
GEORGE DAVIES
when launching Xtend in 1992

People will buy anything that's one to a customer.
SINCLAIR LEWIS

Dear Mr Stevenson, This private invitation is being extended only to you, and a select group of the most respected, successful executives in

the United Kingdom. If you will do us the favour of completing and returning the above certificate, we will immediately ship your FREE *FORTUNE* Pocket Translator.

FORTUNE MAILSHOT

Those who say they are giving the public what it wants begin by underestimating public taste and end by debauching it.

SIR HARRY PILKINGTON
chairman of Pilkington Glass

The public buys its opinions as it buys its milk, on the principle that it is cheaper to do this than keep a cow. So it is, but the milk is more likely to be watered.

SAMUEL BUTLER

My grandfather was a great man. I will follow in his footsteps.

ALESSANDRA MUSSOLINI

1993

Never do business with an Australian who says 'no worries' a lot.

FRANK MOORHOUSE

Room Service

Are you wondering if we have plans to sell prawn sandwiches?

MIKE DAVIES

Prudential executive

on Marks and Spencer's new life and pension operation

If I was in this business for the business, I wouldn't be in business.

SOL HUROK

on plans to bring 532 members of the Bolshoi Ballet to the USA

A dynamic or frightened manager can dramatically improve the short-term profit picture by firing all the research and development staff and so postpone his own eclipse.

T.S. McLEOD

in *Management of Research, Development and Design in Industry*

Becoming indispensable in the workings of a job makes you irreplaceable – and unpromotable.

> HILARY SIMPSON
> Personnel Officer for Oxford County Council
> quoted in *She*

Are you lonely? Hate having to make decisions? Rather talk about it than do it? Then why not hold a meeting? You can get to see other people, offload decisions, impress your colleagues with diagrams on the overhead projector, feel important. And all in work time! MEETINGS – today's alternative to work.

> ANONYMOUS FAX THAT WENT THE ROUNDS IN THE
> EARLY 1990s

We just spray anyone guilty of negative thinking with Neg-repel.

> ANDREW COHN
> chief executive of Betterware

Keeping a secret from him is like sneaking the dawn past a rooster.

> FRED ALLEN
> of his old friend, George Burns

Give him enough rope and he'll hang you.

> Traditional, attributed to SAM GOLDWYN

The National Academy of Sciences people found that only 25 percent of the ingredients people were paying their hard-earned money for could actually be shown to live up to their claims. There was no scientific proof of effectiveness for the rest.

> JOE GRAEDON
> on over-the-counter drugs
> *The People's Pharmacy*

Last June, Fisons took 40 doctors on a three-day free break to the £130-a-night Grosvenor Hotel in Chester. They spent time playing golf, clay pigeon shooting or test-driving four-wheel-drive vehicles. In the evenings they dined on a river showboat and took part in wine tasting.

> *The Sunday Times*
> November 1993

I would be concerned if the company has done anything that is either irregular or indeed illegal.

> LORD PLUMB
> non-executive director of Fisons

We have to have people who are independent. That is especially valid when dealing with the pharmaceutical industry. We do not want people to be tempted to accept free dinners.

> FERNAND SAUER
> chief executive of the EC's pharmaceutical section
> on £80,000 p.a. salaries for deputy directors

Never underestimate drug companies.
> JOE GRAEDON
> *The People's Pharmacy*

It is easy to overlook the absence of appreciable advance in an industry. Inventions that are not made, like babies that are not born, are rarely missed.
> J.K. GALBRAITH

One minute you think you've cracked it, then something else comes up.
> HENRY KIRKUP
> National Criminal Intelligence Service
> executive
> of a new machine that makes watermarking
> cheap and simple

Absolutely everything we do in life is to get love or to compensate for some lack of love. Abraham Maslow has said that the measure of mental health is a person's ability to enter into long-term, intimate, loving relationships with others.
> BRIAN TRACY
> American executive motivator

All our dreams come true – if we have the courage to pursue them.
> WALT DISNEY

Short term, we are not generating enough cash to cover the debt-servicing.

> STEVEN BURKE
> executive vice-president, operations, at Euro Disney

We believe the company has the potential to generate a lot more cash than we are currently generating.

> MIKE MONTGOMERY
> finance director of Euro Disney

I wish all my [sell] calls were as good as Euro Disney. But you are talking to a man who once put out a buy note on Queen's Moat.

> NIGEL REED OF BANQUE PARIBAS
> author in November 1992 of *Euro Disney – a Sell Story*

What could they possibly do with it if they closed it down? What can you do with a second-hand pirate ship?

> JEAN SAMUELS
> Investment consultant

Disney will do all it can to save Euro Disney, but it will not strangle itself. It will not throw £2-billion at Euro Disney.

> SPOKESMAN FOR BANQUE PARIBAS

It's not whether you win or lose, it's how you shift the blame.

BBC EXECUTIVE
during periodic restructuring turmoil

Management consultants are people who borrow your watch to tell you what time it is, and then walk off with it.

ROBERT TOWNSEND

Your social intelligence – your ability to get along with others – is the single most valuable asset you have. Eighty-five percent of what you accomplish in life will be a direct result of how well you get along with others.

BRIAN TRACY
executive motivator

Each generation imagines itself to be more intelligent than the one that went before it, and wiser than the one that comes after it.

GEORGE ORWELL

A good deal of superciliousness
Is based on biliousness.
People seem proud as peacocks
Of any infirmity, be it hives or dementia
    praecox.

OGDEN NASH

Nobody ever forgets where he buried the hatchet.

KIM HUBBARD

Our friends show us what we can do; our enemies teach us what we must do.

GOETHE

Cities are full of people with whom a certain degree of contact is useful and enjoyable, but you do not want them in your hair. And they do not want you in theirs.

JANE JACOBS

Men are more ready to offend one who desires to be beloved than one who wishes to be feared.

NICCOLÒ MACHIAVELLI
Il Principe

Power is the ultimate aphrodisiac.

HENRY KISSINGER
1976

Man is an animal that makes bargains; no other animal does this.

ADAM SMITH

I am just a craftsman, an artisan. The nuts and bolts of solving problems are what interest me.

JACQUES DELORS
1985

Just when you think you've got the rat race licked – Boom! Faster rats.

DAVID LEE ROTH

If you want a job done fast, give it to a busy executive. He'll get his secretary to do it.

TREVOR TURNBULL

Ladbroke Group utilities adviser

Passion persuades. More than intellectual debate, more than reasoning, more than bloody strategy plans.

ANITA RODDICK

chief executive of the Body Shop

Executive ability is a talent for deciding something quickly, and getting someone else to do it.

THOMAS FULLER

THE STRENUOUS LIFE.

There are severe limitations on the amount of information that we are able to receive, process, and remember.

> GEORGE MILLER
> psychologist at Rockefeller University

Glutting a person with more information than he can process may ... lead to disturbance.

> DR JAMES G. MILLER
> University of Michigan

Our report of the Court of Appeal's decision to grant Mr Sulaiman al-Adsani leave to serve writs for compensation on the Kuwaiti government abbreviated the full name of one of the individuals mentioned at the hearing, Sheikh Jaber al Sabah al Saud al Sabah, to Sheik Jaber-al-Sabah ... should not be confused with His Excellency Sheikh Jaber Humoud al Jabah al Sabah, who is also brother-in-law of the Emir of Kuwait.

> *DAILY TELEGRAPH*

Managers plagued by demands for rapid, incessant and complex decisions ... may well find their ability to think and act clearly impaired by the waves of information crashing on their senses.

> ALVIN TOFFLER
> *Future Shock*, 1975

When a man has reached a condition in which he believes that a thing must happen because he does not wish it, and that what he wishes to happen never will be, this is really the state called *desperation*.

ARTHUR SCHOPENHAUER

If I get a prison sentence, I will be the first person to be jailed for generosity. I have been very foolish and very generous all my life.

JOHN POULSON
architectural executive
before collecting a seven-year sentence for
fraud and bribery

I like them to look me in the eye, showing confidence – otherwise it's difficult to gauge how long it will take for them to become confident.

CAROLINE CHARLES
fashion designer

If you're naturally kind you attract a lot of people you don't like.

WILLIAM FEATHER
humorist

Derek is not a colourful figure. He's not what you'd call a *bon vivant*. But he is a strong character, and he's been one of the few to stand up to James [Goldsmith] over the years.

> RUSSELL EDEY
> managing director of N.M. Rothschild
> on Derek Bonham, deputy chairman of Hanson

Whenever I consider promoting anyone, I try to make sure they're up to it. You have to face the fact that some people get to a point where their promotability has reached its limit.

> LUCILLE LEWIN
> chief executive of Whistles chain of boutiques

We expect people to turn their hand to a variety of tasks at a moment's notice and work long hours, including evenings and weekends.

> SARAH GILBERT
> marketing director at Clarins

Keeping on an ineffective man is unfair to him, turning him into a parasite, keeping him from another job where he could contribute more.

> ROBERT TOWNSEND

I am definitely staying. Queen's Moat is a company with a very good future.

> DAVID HOWELL
> MP
> seven days before leaving the company

The ultimate result of shielding men from the effects of folly is to fill the world with fools.

HERBERT SPENCER

The tragedy of executive life is that so many have the ambition, but so few have the ability.

SHELBY FRIEDMAN

Do something. Either lead, follow, or get out of the way!'

EDGAR J. SHALTON

When you start skinning your customers, you should leave some skin on to grow so that you can skin them again.

NIKITA KHRUSHCHEV
Former leader of the USSR

Even in a declaration of war one observes the rules of politeness.

OTTO VON BISMARCK

Severities should be dealt out all at once, that by their suddenness they may give less offence; benefits should be handed out drop by drop, that they may be relished the more.

NICCOLÒ MACHIAVELLI

One cannot walk through a mass-production factory and not feel that one is in Hell.

W.H. AUDEN

With an evening coat and a white tie, anybody, even a stockbroker, can gain a reputation for being civilised.

OSCAR WILDE

The aristocracy created by business rarely settles in the midst of the manufacturing population which it directs; the object is not to govern that population, but to use it.

ALEXIS DE TOCQUEVILLE

To ruin those who possess something is not to come to the aid of those who possess nothing; it is merely to render misery more general.

KLEMENS VON METTERNICH

Thou shalt not covet, but tradition
Approves all forms of competition.

ARTHUR HUGH CLOUGH

To have a good enemy, choose a friend; he knows where to strike.

DIANE DE POITIERS

Love your enemies by all means; it makes them wonder what deal you are trying to put together.

ANON

Have you ever noticed how much easier it is to forgive your enemy after you have got even with him?

STEPHEN LEACOCK

A wise man knows everything. A successful man knows everybody.

AMERICAN PROVERB

We're thrilled they're out and feel it's a good subject for a film — young girls overseas who run into trouble with drugs. I think parents everywhere will be interested.

ADAM FIELDS
executive
on Columbia Pictures' decision to buy the story
of two convicted drug smugglers

When a man is trying to sell you something, don't imagine he is that polite all the time.

EDGAR WATSON HOWE
1911
quoted in *Awake!*

When directors complain about prices today, you can be sure of one thing — they are buying, not selling.

ANON

The skilled executive can negotiate in such a way that all the parties believe that they have won the largest slice of the cake.

LEWIS MANDELBAUM

'A bad bargain!' says the buyer to the seller, but off he goes to brag about it.

PROVERBS 20:14

Make every bargain clear and plain
That none may afterwards complain.
PROVERB

If I'm feeling ill at ease, unhappy, discontented for some reason, chances are 80% to 90% that it's psychological.
BRIAN TRACY
The Phoenix Seminar

Sure I eat what I advertise. Sure I eat wheaties for breakfast. A good bowl of wheaties with bourbon can't be beat.
DIZZ DEAN
on sponsorship

A successful executive is one who delegates all the responsibility, shifts all the blame, and takes all the credit.
WILLIAM HEADS
Exeter businessman

An honest executive is one who shares the credit with the person who did all the work.
E.C. McKENZIE
Economist

When the white man came, we had the land and they had the Bibles. Now they have the land and we have the Bibles.
CHIEF DAN GEORGE

The meek shall inherit the earth, but not the mineral rights.

J. PAUL GETTY

The meek shall inherit the world, but they'll never increase market share.

WILLIAM McGOWAN
chairman of MCI Communications

Market share without profit is like breathing air without oxygen. It feels OK for a while, but in the end it kills you.

ROGER ENRICO
of Pepsico Worldwide Beverages

I think I might have mentioned the other week, by way of a sullen antidote to the *Saturday Review*'s Stars and Stripes Forever special, how stupid the average American is, I forgot to add: and ignorant, too.

JOHN DIAMOND
Saturday Review

Operating in America is like swimming in a shark pool. When you do that from 5,000 miles away, you can get eaten alive.

GERALD RONSON
Chairman of Heron Group
after diversifying into America and losing
£230m

I don't believe you can run a major US company from abroad. George III tried to run the United States from Britain, and look what happened to him.

SIR GORDON WHITE
chairman of Hanson Industries Inc.

Ungexoshe mpalambili.
(You cannot chase two antelope at once.)

ZULU PROVERB

We tend to meet any new situation by reorganisation and attribute to this the illusion that progress is being made.

PETRONIUS ARBITER
who committed suicide 66 AD

The best way to slow progress in a company is to form a committee to do something about it.

AMERICAN PROVERB

Teamwork consists of a lot of people doing what I say.

MATTHEW FURNEAUX
Sun Life

Now listen slowly.

QUOTED BY DAVID SIBREY OF IBSA
on group presentations

A holding company is a thing where you hand an accomplice the goods while the policeman searches you.

WILL ROGERS
American comedian

An arrant individualist, selfish, narrow-minded, quite blandly antisocial, he went after whatever he sought and took it by fair means or foul – and whoever didn't like it was welcome to a battle.

KENNETH W. PORTER
on John J. Astor, 1st Baron Astor of Hever, son of the 1st Viscount Astor, MP and proprietor of *The Times*

Warning to all business executives who occasionally tell little white lies – before you employ a secretary, check her religion. A prominent City figure, called to the telephone to speak to someone he was trying to avoid, told his temporary secretary: 'Tell him I'm busy and that I'll call him back later.' He couldn't believe his ears when she replied: 'I can't tell lies – I'm a Jehovah's Witness.'

THE TIMES

The day of the yes-man is over. Does everybody agree?

CHIEF EXECUTIVE OF A MILWAUKEE COMPANY

Commerce, which ought naturally to be, among nations, as among individuals, a bond of union and friendship, has become the most fertile source of discord and animosity.

ADAM SMITH
The Wealth of Nations

It's too late to agree with me. I've already changed my mind.

SIGN ON CHICAGO EXECUTIVE'S DESK

If it had been a really good idea, I would have thought of it first.

ANON

It's a wonderful book, and when you consider for $22.50 you would only be able to purchase a couple of pairs of knickers and a tin whistle I recommend buying this bargain instead.

AUSTRALIAN REVIEW OF *THE OXFORD ILLUSTRATED HISTORY OF BRITAIN*

Must we stand with one foot on the neck of the vanquished in order to be happy?

PSYCHOLOGY AND LIFE

Beatus ille, qui procul negotiis,
Ut prisca gens mortalium,
Paterna rura bubus exercet suis,
Solutus omni faenore.

(Happy the executive who can get away from the negotiating table to dabble in a bit of DIY ploughing on a mortgage-free family farm, with no bank manager on his back.)

> HORACE
> 68–5 BC

Divided duties are seldom split in the middle.

> HENRY S. HASKINS

There's one thing to be said for inviting trouble: it generally accepts.

> MAE MALOO
> 1976

Are you sitting comfortably? Then I'll begin.

> JULIA LANG ON *LISTEN WITH MOTHER*
> and traditional opening of post-lunch board meetings

The chief cause of problems is solutions.

> PAUL DICKSON
> *The Official Rules*
> 1978

Smart leaders … know they're going to be wrong a certain percent of the time. That's why they *want* these opposing points of view – to cut down on mistakes before they are made, and to correct past errors as promptly as possible.

> *BITS AND PIECES*

The average executive doesn't think he is.
NICK FURNEAUX
Bristol marketing executive

The average executive is forty-two around the chest, forty-four around the house, ninety-six around the golf course, and a nuisance around the office.
ROBERT REID

I exchange abusive letters with my competitors on a regular basis.
STEVE ATKINS
Scotlife Home Loans

The best executives are those with the sense enough to pick the right people for the job, and then let them get on with it.
PAUL MILLER

He meddles constantly. He is seldom to be found at his desk. He is usually up to his elbows in a dismantled motor and while the man who should be doing the work stands watching, other workmen sit around waiting to be assigned new tasks. As a result, the shop is always overcrowded with work, always in a muddle, and delivery times are often missed.
DR LAURENCE J. PETER

We few, we happy few, we band of brothers,
For he, today, that sheds his blood with me
Shall be my brother …
> WILLIAM SHAKESPEARE
> *Henry V*, act IV

It's common to find that people who claim they are overworked are hanging on to parts of the job they could delegate. They can't let go.
> HILARY SIMPSON
> Personnel Officer for Oxford County Council

Behind every successful executive there's a woman telling him he's not so hot.
> AMERICAN PROVERB

Man seeks to acquire a rank among his fellow men, whom he detests, but without whom he cannot live.
> IMMANUEL KANT

If anyone wants their ingrowing toenail or gallstones removed, I am now a senior consultant as well as an actuary.
> JOHN JENKINS
> Alexander Clay and Partners

Chronic anger is so damaging to the body that it ranks with, or even exceeds, cigarette smoking, obesity and a high-fat diet as a powerful risk factor for early death.
> *THE NEW YORK TIMES*

In 1987 in Japan sudden deaths of top business executives in their 40s, 50s and 60s jumped to three times that of the same period the previous year. Their deaths were attributed to 'unimaginable stress' that accompanies the post of today's top executives ... harsh business conditions aggravated by inflation contributed to their stressful life. [Japan's] Federation of Employers' Association has issued eight rules to prevent stress. The rules include: Avoid hard schedules, exercising more than thirty minutes every day, and laughing.

MAINICHI DAILY NEWS

Tokyo

Laughter is the cheapest luxury a businessman has. It stirs up the blood, expands the chest, electrifies the nerves, clears away the cobwebs from the brain, and gives the whole system, a general rehabilitation.

E.C. McKENZIE

Money, achievement, fame, and success are important, but they are bought too dearly when acquired at the cost of health.

ANON

550 million workdays are lost each year in the United States because workers suffer pain of one kind or another. Headaches topped the list with 157 million workdays lost. Bone-joint

pains of various kinds ranked second with 108 million lost workdays. Then followed 99 million workdays lost for stomach pains, 89 million for backaches, 58 million for muscle pains, 28 million for menstrual pains, and 15 million for dental pains.

NUPRIN PAIN REPORT
1987

Executive success is achieved by yearning, learning and earning.

ANON

He who makes a fortune by telling lies runs needlessly into the toils of death.

PROVERBS 21:6 (New English Bible)

A top executive of the Japanese National Railway (JNR) chose resignation rather than separation from his family ... Says Tamura, 'The job of the director general can be taken by anybody. But only I am the father of my children.'

MAINICHI DAILY NEWS

Though mothers and fathers give us life, it is money alone which preserves it.

IHARA SAIKUKU
The Millionaires' Gospel

You can have anything you want – if you want it badly enough. You can be anything you want to be, have anything you desire, accomplish anything you set out to accomplish – if you hold to that desire with singleness of purpose.

ROBERT COLLIER

You've got more crooks on Wall Street than in any other industry I've ever seen.

LOUIS WOLFSON

It is a part of the social mission of every great newspaper to provide a refuge and a home for the largest possible number of salaried eccentrics.

LORD THOMSON OF FLEET

He only listens when he's talking.

ALAN LEVY
of Simon Wiesenthal

83

Most people give up just when they're about to achieve success. They quit on the one-yard line. They give up at the last minute of the game one foot from a winning touchdown.

> H. ROSS PEROT
> billionaire business executive, who withdrew
> from the US presidential election

How badly do you want it, and are you prepared to pay the price?

> PETER TURGOOSE
> formerly top manager of Allied Dunbar

There is no pleasure in winning money from a man who does not feel it.

> LORD HOUGHTON
> Victorian biographer

Never complain, never explain.

> HENRY FORD

Maynard Keynes was to economics what his cousin Milton was to town planning.

> PAUL STEVENSON

We are becoming so comfortable with talking to a machine that we are losing the ability to communicate with other people.

> GERRY HANSON
> chairman of the Polite Society

It's just computers selling to computers.
> THE NEW YORK TIMES
> of Black Monday 19 October 1987, when stock
> brokers worldwide lost control of the market

We have created a gigantic financial house of cards. We have had fair warning about its weakness.
> FELIX ROHATYN
> American merchant bank executive

He who has his thumb on the purse has the power.
> OTTO VON BISMARK
> in a speech to the Prussian Diet, 1869

I really feel that if you can trade one market, you can trade them all. The principles are the same. Trading is emotion. It is mass psychology, greed and fear. It is all the same in every situation.
> JACK D. SCHWAGER
> NY market expert

You always get something of value out of Marty Zweig. He is very solid.
> MICHAEL MARCUS
> Commodities Corporation top trader
> of the author of *The Zweig Letter*, Baltimore,
> NY

If I wanted to become a tramp, I would seek information and advice from the most success-

ful tramp I could find. If I wanted to become a
failure, I would seek advice from men who had
never succeeded. If I wanted to succeed in all
things, I would look around me for those who
are succeeding and do as they have done.

> JOSEPH MARSHALL WADE
> quoted in *Treasury of Wall Street Wisdom*
> edited by Harry D. Schulz and Samson Coslow

Seedy little men.

> KELVIN McKENZIE
> of Mirror Group executives
> shortly before becoming one, in charge of
> Group TV interests

The new establishment is not a meritocracy,
but a power elite of money-shifters, middle-men
and speculators.

> TONY BLAIR
> at the Labour Party conference, October 1994

We work in the dark – we do what we can – we
give what we have. Our doubt is our passion,
and our passion is our task.

> HENRY JAMES
> in his autobiography, *The Middle Years*

Even mediocre people can shoulder responsibility.

> HELMUT SCHMIDT
> German minister of finance 1972–4

Follow your desire as long as you live and do not perform more than is ordered ... when riches are gained, follow desire, for riches will not benefit if one is sluggish.

THE MAXIMS OF PTAHHOTPE, *c.* 2352 BC

I wanted him to be the kind of man who had never walked along the beach and felt the grass under his feet.

BILL FORSYTH
quoted in *Colemanballs 2*

It doesn't feel like work, except when you lose – then it feels like work.

BRUCE KOVNER
Interbank currency trader at Commodities Corporation

You've got to learn how to fall, before you learn to fly.

PAUL SIMON
Song writer

One of [life's pleasures] is simply sitting still, like a snake on a sun-warmed stone, with a delicious sense of indolence that was seldom enjoyed in earlier years.

MALCOLM COWLEY
American literary historian at 80

My guiding star always is, Get hold of portable property.
>   CHARLES DICKENS
>   *Great Expectations*

A minute's success pays the failure of years.
>   ROBERT BROWNING
>   *Apollo and the Fates*, 1886

Make no little plans; they have no magic to stir men's blood.
>   DANIEL HUDSON BURNHAM (1846–1912)
>   chief of construction for Chicago World Fair

Corporate warriors are haunted by the nightmare of karoshi, or death from overwork. A lawyer specializing in such cases estimates that there are at least 30,000 victims of karoshi in Japan every year.
>   MAINICHI DAILY NEWS
>   Tokyo, 1994

Criticism is often given in generalities … Requesting particulars will enable you to find out exactly what the other person's objections are … Like a reporter, all you do is pose questions designed to find out who, what, when, where, why, and how.
>   ALAN GARNER
>   *Conversationally Speaking*

If [company executives] are already plagued by self-criticism, we will be particularly troubled when we get criticism from others. Even if someone praises us and has only one small thing to criticize, we usually zero in on the inadequacy more than on the things we do well.

DR HAROLD BLOOMFIELD
US author and counsellor

One who is serious all day will never have a good time, while one who is frivolous all day will never establish a household.

THE MAXIMS OF PTAHHOTPE

Hegel says somewhere that all great events and personalities in world history reappear in one fashion or another. He forgot to add: the first time as tragedy, the second as farce.

KARL MARX

Let's just say Richie ran that four hundred bucks up pretty good.

RICHARD DENNIS'S FATHER
on his commodity trading executive son's
turning $400 into $200 million

We must involve our peoples in a greater appreciation of the need for change; change in expectations about growth and earnings, change in management ... change in the pattern of industry.

OTTAWA DECLARATION 1984

It is a little bit like playing golf: You can throw your clubs around after making a bad shot, but while you are making your next shot you should keep your head down and keep your eye on the ball.

> RICHARD DENNIS
> former trading executive whose managed
> public funds made massive losses in 1987–88

Apart from work, of course, what really turns me on is clay pigeon shooting, paint-balling, really big banquets, treasure hunts, off-track rallying and suet puddings with jam in the middle. And you can't get those things at the Corporation leisure centre.

> ALLIED DUNBAR EXECUTIVE
> on why corporate hospitality in stately homes
> was justified in a recession

There is no way these [stately] homes will survive without ... the companies that hold conferences and social events in them. They are the life blood of historic houses, keeping the bailiffs at bay.

> THE EARL OF BRADFORD
> *Stately Secrets*

One would have thought by now we had moved away from the idea that real fraud must be about ruining widows and orphans and in some way, shape or form commercial fraud might somehow be victimless. It is not.

JUDGE GEOFFREY RIVLIN QC
at the Brent Walker trial

The top salesmen in any field are hyperactive for four months of the year, unable to sit still or sleep because they want to get on with what they are doing. For two months of the year they are treading water, miserable, sleeping badly, worrying where the next result will come from. For the other six months of the year they vacillate between the two states, awake at night trying to work out how they can break out of mediocrity and be a star again. Either way you don't sleep much, because that sort of success is all-consuming.

SIMON MONTGOMERY
Executive recruiter

Mr Mavrodi spent two months in prison while his pyramid business was investigated on charges of tax evasion and fraud. He is now running for a seat in Parliament and immunity from prosecution.

NEWS REPORT
on Sergei Mavrodi, chief executive of MMM in Moscow, 1994

Good investing is really just common sense. But it is astonishing how few people have common sense.

> JAMES B. ROGERS, JUN
> who formed the Quantum Fund with George Soros
> in an interview with Jack D. Schwager in *Market Wizards*

We put applicants for senior engineering jobs through the coffee test: if they can open a tetrapack without getting milk on their ties, they're in.

> JOHN LAMBERT
> DVH Chemicals executive

Burnout has no precise definition, but the commonly accepted symptoms include fatigue, low morale, absenteeism, increased health problems, and drug or alcohol abuse.

> *FORTUNE* MAGAZINE

I like to work long hours, but if you have to lose your husband or your family in the process, you're doing things the wrong way. It's no fun to count your money by yourself.

> MARY KAY ASH
> Chairman, Mary Kay Cosmetics

Any type of useful activity in which one feels a sense of accomplishment or of doing something worthwhile can make retirement meaningful.

DR ROBERT BUTLER
of the National Institute on Ageing

In our society ... so strong is the link between work, self-esteem and social position that, on retirement, some executives find it extremely difficult to adjust to a life free of their former roles ... Those who center their lives on work must ask themselves this question: 'What will I have left if my work is taken away?'

AT WORK
Corporate guidance book

If your husband loses his appetite, suffers sleeplessness, refuses to talk, then he is sending warning signals. Tell him to find pleasure in something other than work and try to meet non-company people.

DR TORU SEKIYA
Executive consultant
Sekiya Neurology Clinic, Tokyo

I had a great struggle with myself. Tears flooded my eyes several times.

LORD REITH
Founder of the BBC
Diaries
on being sacked from Cabinet by Winston Churchill and losing his chauffeured car

Before retiring early from executive life, take a week off and watch daytime television.

SUREWATER NEWSLETTER

Retirement at sixty-five is ridiculous. When I was sixty-five I still had pimples.

GEORGE BURNS

They just threw me out on the … street. I put 30 guys away, six of them bosses, and now the whole world is looking for me. I'm 74 years old. Where am I going to find work at my age?

ALADENA 'JIMMY THE WEASEL' FRATIANNO
Mafia executive executioner turned informer,
who died in his sleep at 79

Never felt better.

NORMAN LAMONT
one hour before being sacked as Chancellor of
the Exchequer

I left the room with silent dignity, but caught my foot in the mat.

GEORGE AND WEEDON GROSSMITH
Diary of a Nobody

Now that Nigel isn't running Trafalgar, it's important for us not to see too much of each other, so I shoot him out of the door every morning.

LADY BROACKES
of Sir Nigel Broackes following his retirement
as chairman of Trafalgar House